POSITIVE
IN LOVE AND LIGHT

Daily Positive Words

VOLUME 1

Dear Elizabeth,
Hope you enjoy
Love & Light

Lesley McKeever

ORIGINAL WRITING

ISBN
978-1-78237-000-0

A CIP catalogue for this book is available from the National Library.

Published by ORIGINAL WRITING LTD., Dublin,
2012.

Printed by CLONDALKIN GROUP, Glasnevin, Dublin 11

Today I take control of my thoughts and actions. I no longer hold the need to be negative. I know I am one with my body, mind and soul. I will now move forward to create and to live the life I desire.

Everything in your life will be exactly how you see everything in your life.

YOUR CHOICE!

Love and light Les 2012

Inspire your day with the power of positive Words and reflection.

From "Soul Angel and Energy Healing"

To my wonderful little foot, Madison Marie:
You came into my life and changed it forever. Your light, your
love, your soul are always an inspiration to me. I love you for
you, always and forever just as you are.
I make this journey for us now. I LOVE YOU.

To Mom and Dad.
Not always did I listen, not always agreed. As my age grows my
eyes now see. How amazing your teachings are. How much I
have learnt and how much I truly owe to you both. I love you!

To my dear friends you know who you are; you are all a divine
gift that I will cherish for eternity. And not just for each of your
sublime editing skills. Especially Leonora and Dave. Thank
you!

To God and the all the Angels and Saints of Heaven, for their ever loving presence and guidance, thank you for my very first book! Amen

To all those divine angels on Soul Angel and Energy Healing who inspire and connect so brightly, thank you for your constant love and belief in the journey of life and spiritual growth.

Love and Light, Les!

CONTENTS

INTRODUCTION

This is the tiny yet powerful pocket book of hope and inspiration. All you do is ask your Angels and God *(Higher Power, God, Universe, as and what you believe that to be for you)* for help as you close your eyes, breathe deep and flick through the pages. Trust your gut instinct and the page you land on is your word of positivity that will echo through you and your day. You can use this as often as you like. Each word has a simple explanation to help you reflect and think about what that word means for you today. Some people pick a word daily, others by the week. You will know when it is right for you. Whenever you feel the need or would like to... just flick through the pages again. Trust me; this mini affirmation will do you wonders. The main thing is, just enjoy the guidance and light. Today you are choosing to make you happy and listen to your soul sing. Shine and be bright in the wonder that is you xxx.

✿ چگ ِ ⌢ ˜ ♡ *Love&Light*

LOVE

I feel that this word is aimed within. A gentle reminder that you need to find yourself: enjoy and love you, before you can truly love and guide others around you. Give yourself loving words daily. Compliment yourself. See all the wonderful gifts that make up the angelic soul that you are. Live in gratitude and above all live in love for you and your world. Love shared with others is a cherished gift that comes from the heavenly bond you share with you and with others. From this true LOVE of self you will shine and grow.

✿ *Love & Light*

STRENGTH

You are enough. You are the answer. Everything you need is right inside you and always has been. You are being asked to take a minute to look within and see all of your strengths. You have any answer you need if you take the time to trust, look and listen to your gut/voice within. Just ask God and the Angels and they will help you see your beauty and STRENGTH within. Never hold fear as this will cloud your judgment. Hold faith and belief in yourself and all will work out for the best.

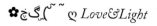 ❀ ♡ *Love&Light*

SHINE

This is very powerful and aimed right within.
You are being asked to shine with all the gifts you
have already and the ones you are learning. You
have all you need right inside you, it always has
been there. You need to see that, feel that, love that
and just be that. Then you will shine to all and for
yourself and those dreams you have. They are in
your hand if you just shine. It is time to love you
and let go of fear. Hand your life over to God
daily and ask for help and/or guidance if you find
it hard to shine. Once you ask the help will come.
Self confidence is the key; it is your time to shine so
SHINE bright xxx

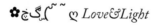 *Love&Light*

REMEMBER

This is a gift we all hold and share. We also control what we choose to remember. Memories should be held in the greatest of love and light. Holding on to any negatives serves no purpose. Once you have learnt a lesson that is where it should stay. A learning post not a hitching post; you have the power to choose what you REMEMBER. Remember things that serve your purpose going forward in life. If it is with a lost loved one, remember that in memory no one has really left us.

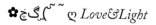 ~ ♡ *Love&Light*

TOLERANT

Most feel that this is something they must feel for the outside world and in the long run I suppose it is. However for the now this is for you. It is a warm hug to remind you to go easy on yourself. Try and take a hold of negative self talk that can sneak in from time to time. Allow for mistakes, learn from them and let them go in the knowledge that you will do better next time. Love yourself and start being thankful and TOLERANT of you. Then that tolerance will be for others. Because if we are not tolerant of others the reason is within, it is something about us we don't like. So save the time and start to love yourself as God loves you.

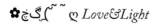 ♥ *Love&Light*

WIND

This is a very earthly word. A double meaning really; it tends to mean get out into the air, feel the wind on your skin. Let it blow away your worries and thoughts. Let the wind bring you into the place of just being. Stand still and enjoy that moment and within that moment, you will find what you were looking for. Let the feeling of just being be the wind that lets you soar, raise you up to be all you can be. You will find your driving force or WIND while standing in nature's driving force of divine wind.

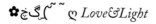 *Love&Light*

OPEN

This is a gentle nudge for you to trust your soul and gut. To know that you are strong and what you feel is valid. You need to open up to other viewpoints and beliefs. Only when you open can you allow true and unconditional love to enter. You will also get to know yourself more when you open your body, mind and soul. Open up to the leap of faith and hand your day or any situation over to God. Open up to the abundance and love that is around you and already within you: OPEN to your inner power.

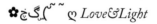 *Love&Light*

PEACE

Peace is yours for the taking; it is in fact a natural state within you. Looking within and listening to your inner state will lead you to your divine peace, release the need to look elsewhere or outside you for peace! True and tranquil peace is found within. Your true state, your inner knowledge, when listened to, will always guide your body, mind, heart and soul back to a state of peace. Peace is a gift you receive from you, when you accept you as you are and accept the knowledge that all is as it should be; you are doing your best. When you take time to JUST BE, stopping the chitter chatter of negative thoughts in the brain, to live in the moment, happiness and release will follow, leaving your true self in a state of peace. You are being asked to take time daily to follow your inner guidance to your state of peace, rely on no outside source to make you happy. Being truly happy with you is true peace. All is safe and just as it should be, find PEACE in that knowledge and release.

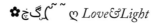 *Love&Light*

LIGHTNING

I always find this one very like listen. You are being asked to look within to help you look to your outside world. What makes you strike like lightning? What burns your eternal fire? It is time to find and follow what you love and dream of; your LIGHTNING will strike, it is your time now.

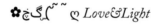 *Love&Light*

ROOTS

Roots is a wonderful word, a reminder of who you are and to ground yourself. Stay steady and true to yourself and remember the true you. Your roots will follow you always so never be afraid to have roots and wings. Trust in you, love you exactly as you are and grow tall through the stable foundation of the ROOTS of your soul. You are amazing so trust yourself and grow.

 *Love&Light*

BLOOM

It is time to shine and shed off any misconceptions that you have about your ability... open your mind and heart like a lotus flower in bloom. You have a divine gift which is now to be shared with the world. You are protected and guided as you move through this magical new growth phase in your life. Be proud, stand tall and BLOOM as the divine being you are.

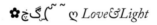 *Love&Light*

PRIDE

Go on, see you for you. Pride is a good thing when it comes from gratitude for who you are and for your gifts. This is a little nudge for you to be proud of all you have achieved and all you are capable of. You were made to be great, so honour your maker and be great. It is ok to take PRIDE and shine.

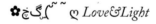 ♥ *Love&Light*

LIGHT

You beam love; you raise the vibrations of others. You are light, you are from light and you can share light. This is to remind you that even in what you may think are the darkest of times, no matter what they may be; your light is still shining. Take time to see within and love yourself. Know everything for you is happening exactly as it should be and you are safe. Release all worry. You are light and were created from light. You are always being guarded and guided by light. It is safe for you to live in LIGHT.

 *Love&Light*

POSITIVE

You have hopes, wishes and dreams. You are being asked to focus on only the things in life that make you happy. Focus on the things you want. Like brings like; positive will bring more positive. The true secret of manifestation is living in gratitude and love for all around you and all you have already. Living in this positive manner will bring you more of the like. Shine bright, think big and always know, you are protected and loved and all will come to you exactly when it should do. You deserve the very best of everything so be POSITIVE and remember this always.

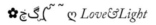 *Love&Light*

HOLD

There are two things that are being whispered to you. HOLD true to yourself, listen to your gut. You must move on from denying your inner voice a chance to shine. You already know what you stand for and what you want; it is time to move towards that and stand up for whom and what you are. Hold true to yourself in honesty and light. Also within your movement you need to hold on and hold your faith. Give all your issues away to God and just sit back in the comfort of faith and belief that all will be ok, hold faith and let God hold you.

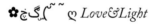 ❁چگ᠋ڡ᠊ ~ ♡ *Love&Light*

LIVE

It is time to cut the crap. God's nice way of saying, you have nothing to fear. Release and stop holding back. You're safe to move on and up. You have all the knowledge, support and power within you. Take control of you so you can live and beam. Be bright, and shine your wonderful God given light that is within you. JUST BE, JUST LIVE!

✿چگڒ˜ ♡ *Love&Light*

RELEASE

For you and your union with your soul it is time to forgive and move: To rise above through release of all negative emotions and feelings. In the long run these only hurt your being and stop you just being. The people or situations you hold these feelings for have no idea you are holding them against them and holding on to them will not change any of the past either. These emotions are a waste of your divine love and light. You are strong and safe; you are so much more than any hurt. Release it all to God and sigh a relief for you and your soul that are now free to soar. RELEASE and you will be free.

❀ چگ ῀ ῀ ♡ *Love&Light*

WATER

The giver of life and powerful force of nature with such a tender and nurturing side: You too are made up of all these wonderful gifts and traits: It is time for you to truly love and work with you. See yourself for the magnificent being that you are... You are just like WATER, ever moving and ever rejuvenating. To help you along with your life purpose, connect with water as often as possible. Drink it to keep your body strong and alert, swim, or paddle in the sea. Whatever way you can, make contact and ground with the source of life and see it as a huge part in the source of your life, let it fuel the radiance and magnificence you can shine.

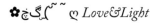 *Love&Light*

SOULMATE

This is a word that leads many to look outside. However, you are being hugged from above with this word. You have found your SOUL MATE; you always knew your soul mate. It is you and your very being. You are being asked to spend time with you, true time. Build your relationship strong and true and be happy with your own company. If a soul mate or twin soul is something you seek on the outside, nothing will attract that more than you being truly happy on the inside. Mates always find each other, in divine timing. So look and work within, knowing that everything on the outside is being taken care of.

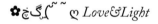 ~ ♡ *Love&Light*

FAIR

Today is the day you are being asked, are you being fair? Are you being good and kind to you? It is time to stop always thinking of the things you think you did wrong. Everything in your life has brought you to where you are now. It has all helped to make you, you. You are being watched and minded. So it is safe for you now to be nice and kind and tolerant of yourself. Starting seeing all the wonderful things that go together to make you: You are a divine being of love and light. So be FAIR to you as you are to others and you will shine even more.

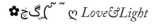 *Love&Light*

REAL

Everything you can dream of is real, everything you want and love is real. All you feel within you deep from your soul is so very real, the power is within you already. Your ability to shine and help others is also real. You are being reminded how wonderful you truly are and to hold true to how REAL your spirituality is. Move off from doubt and second guessing and move into the trust and faith that all is well and perfect in your world and your Divine connection is very real.

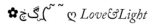 *Love&Light*

SOAR

You are being gently told it is time. Time for you to realise your full potential, time to rise above all fears and negativities, they have no place with you anymore. Rise above those who say no and can't. Your dreams are manifesting as you read this. Spread your divine light and wings so you can SOAR high.

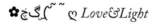 *Love&Light*

AIR

Life giver: Wonder of all being and creation. Without it we cannot live. Your body knows this. So too does your soul. This has a couple of meanings. You need to get out and enjoy the world outside. You need to let your body, mind and soul breathe in the air of life. Enjoy it, let it fill you and motivate you. You are also being told that you are being fed air from above. Inspiration and life air for the soul; find your soul's air, be it by reading, meditation, nature. Whatever works for you, as your body needs air, so does your soul. Be one with your soul, find those happy things, laugh out loud, sing... All these things make you and your soul take in AIR. You will find your natural state of happiness through air.

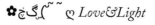 ♥ *Love&Light*

DIVINE

You are divine in the likeness of your maker. You too are a being of unconditional love and light. Stand strong in the divinity of your true self. To love you truly allows you to truly love others. You are being asked to think in your spiritual life, see in your spiritual life. All things around you will change and grow and become clearer as you begin to live as the spiritual wonder that you are. Be the DIVINE you.

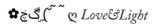 *Love&Light*

BREATHE

Take a moment to stop and just breathe. Just be in the now, just breathe in this moment. Breathe in and inhale God's love and light deep within. Through this breath you will see your true surroundings and all you have to be grateful for. Life is full of gifts and joy but you must remember to see it and feel it. If you are ever confused on how to live always come back to your life giving breath ~ BREATHE and JUST BE

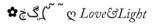 ~ ♡ *Love&Light*

SELF

All the journeys you will choose to take will and need to come from the SELF, even if we are not aware of this. You are being held close and tight in love and light by angels and are being asked to truly see you as they see you. Everything within the self is there, knowledge, trust, power, healing, joy, gratitude, everything. It is all there for you already. You only need to find you, love you and trust you. Take a few moments daily to just BE, getting to know the self is a truly wonderful journey, ups and downs and all. Knowing you, allows you to really know others. You can shine, you are safe. Find your SELF.

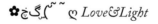 *Love&Light*

LEARN

Everything around is true and real. Everything within you is true and real. Take time daily to see your world, take time to see you, notice the little God winks! (some may call co-incidences). Look at people in your life, people you meet in a funny manner, feathers, all the little things that seem to happen, and when you put them all together you realise that you are being talked to and reminded that you are not alone. Remember to take heed of everything you have experienced, learn from your past. Move from your past in forgiveness and light, taking the new knowledge with you and leaving the lesson where it belongs, in the past. LEARN in all parts of your life, knowledge is a key factor in life that will one day when used correctly, lead to wisdom.

❁ جگٌ˜ ˜ ღ *Love&Light*

EXERCISE

This word means that if you do go outside and take the air or you do engage in exercise your lower thoughts will release. Your ego will rest and your spiritual thoughts and inner knowledge will rise, and so will your vibrations, and through this your answers will come. EXERCISE can give you clarity through pulling the body and mind together in a very powerful union.

❀چگڑم ~ ღ *Love&Light*

VIBRANT

This is a gentle reminder of your likeness to your creator. A reminder of whom and what you are. All you have ever needed is within and still is there. You just need to see it and feel it. You need to shine in the vibrancy of your very being. Gratitude in the moments of the simple things of life will ring this feeling true. Remember that no matter what happens, you are alive, you still want more, and you are you. The vibrant divine being that your creator wanted you to be! So be the VIBRANT you and go forth towards your life purpose.

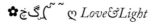 Love&Light

GIVE

This is an outstanding message and guide from above, and a lovely reminder to give to you what you give to others. Give yourself the love, tolerances, kindness, joy, everything that you are so willing to give to others. Try not to forget to love and give to you. Keep that beautiful soul shining and happy and you can give so much more to others too. You also need to make sure that you give yourself a break when needed. Remember to be gentle to you and try not to be too hard on yourself by placing too many should do's and have to's : give yourself the gift of doing things you love to do. You are divine so GIVE yourself the love you deserve.

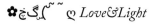 *Love&Light*

MANIFEST

God wants you to take time out to stop and listen to your heart and soul. Listen to your thoughts and try and make sure that you are only thinking thoughts you want to happen. The power to bring your dreams alive is within you. Your thoughts create your tomorrow. Spend time around things you love, people you love and do things that you love to do. See your world and tune in to all the little things that join together to give you signs and guidance from above and within. MANIFEST the life you want now, believe in your ability to manifest. You are manifesting with every thought you create so make sure your thoughts are creating the manifestations of your dreams.

✿ ﺝ ﮒ ⌢ ˜ ♡ *Love&Light*

AWAKEN

It is time to see you, it is time to shine. You have a soul that is wise and strong; you are always divinely protected and guided. Little parts of you are calling out, so it is time to honour those parts of you that will guide you to your life purpose. Trust in your gut: that is your wisdom and God talking to you. Believe in love and light and shine yours brightly. Awaken every inch of your soul and spiritual being. From now on you will be you and see the world from a point of AWAKENING.

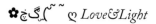 *Love&Light*

RIGHTS

As you go through your spiritual life be sure to stay true to you. You may feel more empathy; feel closer and more obliged to help all. This is a hand in hand process of spiritual growth, but you must remember you and your right not to help if needs be or if something is not sitting with you. This holds very strongly with being true to your right to be happy, to have your dreams come true. Remember the power for all that is in love and light is within you, and that is not only your greatest gift but is one of your God-given RIGHTS.

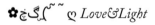 *Love&Light*

FRIENDS

Friends are a wonderful gift and huge source of comfort and love. However, in the spirit of true happiness, to truly have friends we must be truly friends with ourselves. Be kind to you, enjoy you. Share happy times and day dream. Become true FRIENDS with the soul of you: For when you truly make you happy, others that you will be happy with and want around you will draw near to your shine.

❀ۄڒڒۘ ˜˜ ლ *Love&Light*

CARPE DIEM

Need more be said?

✿چگ⁀ˆ˜ ℘ *Love&Light*

SURROUNDED

This is one of the strongest signs that you are never alone, not only are you SURROUNDED on earth by loved ones but you are divinely protected and guided always. You have a heavenly chorus with you at the moment strongly leading you forward in your life. Now is the time to take the chances, live the dreams and be all you can be. You are safe and surrounded inside and outside. Shine on; knowing that as you shine, you surround yourself in love which is the likeness of your Divine creator and your Divine creator is surrounding you in love.

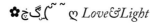 *Love&Light*

ACHIEVE

You hold the power of all you desire within you. You can achieve anything you believe in. Nothing is too great or too small. Hold strong in your faith, your faith in you and your faith that everything always works out just as it should do. If you want something, go get it. You have been given all your tools, now, take time to get to know your gifts and talents and love you. Take time to live in gratitude for all you have and you can ACHIEVE anything!

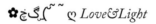 *Love&Light*

PAINT

Creativity is one of the soul's ways of coming through and speaking to you and to the world around you. No matter how you choose to express yourself, you will feel alive and grounded in doing so. The word paint here can of course mean painting literally, however. Paint can also mean paint the world with your creative power and show all your true colours. Create a part of you that is in peace and harmony with your total being, love the true you and PAINT all those around you in your light and love.

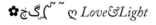 ♥ *Love&Light*

NEST

Your surroundings sometimes mimic your mind. Hugs and light are being sent to you to help you nest well in yourself. Love deep within and see all the wonderful things that others see. Treat yourself with love and compassion. Let your light shine inwards and outwards. Nesting well inside, allows you to NEST well outside.

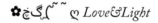 ~ ♡ *Love&Light*

LOOK

You have a wise and loving soul. With this comes the power to truly look. Look within; look beyond, to really look. Let your senses guide you to the truth. When you allow your soul to LOOK you will feel the real meaning of any situation. From now on, grant yourself the gift of really looking.

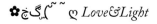 *Love&Light*

WITHIN

Everything you need to know is already within. You are being guided to stop searching the outside world for answers. You are being asked to stop looking to others to make you feel. You have you. From within; loving and knowing who you really are, is all the love and support you will really need. The power is already WITHIN you. Have faith in this and shine from within.

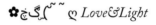 *Love&Light*

FLY

In your being, you are like and at one with your maker. Your dreams are right before and within you, your gifts are your tools. It is all up to you now. Through your faith in you and your maker you can fly now. Fly higher than you ever have before, have no fear this is where you belong. Nothing is too great when placed within faith. FLY now, to and with your dreams.

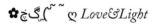 *Love&Light*

LAUGH

Laughter is a pure "In the moment" expression of happiness. Your vibrations soar, your soul beams and your eyes shine. You can carry laughter wherever you go now and always. It can heal in an instant. Laughter can sooth immediately. It can turn yours or someone else's day right around. You are being asked to LAUGH, and laugh whenever you are low, feel your energy radiate and encapsulate you and everyone around you.

✿چگؑ ˜ ♡ Love&Light

MUSIC

Music makes the soul soar, it makes the body dance and it makes the mind sing. You have everything you need right there when it comes to pulling body, mind and soul together. When you are enjoying music you are JUST BEING; as you were divinely created to be! Take note of everything you feel when listening to music you like, this is a huge clue as to how to find the power of JUST BEING every minute of every day. When you are lost in MUSIC the Ego is out, and the body, mind and soul as one, is in. You will achieve everything with this show of true gratitude to all that you are as one.

 *Love&Light*

PRAYER

Prayer means many things to many different people. But prayer in itself is the same thing. It is the time when you are truly honest, it is the time when you show the real you and give gratitude or ask for help. You are being held close and reminded to get in touch with whatever prayer means to you. Talk and open up so you can feel and heal. You are being watched but they cannot help if you do not ask, and that's where the prayer comes in. Not only is it the plea for help or praise in gratitude ringing out, it gives you time to think and hear your thoughts clearly, you will be in touch with you in PRAYER and grounded. And from these places is the start of all the wonders of your life. Lift up, talk to you, talk to God and enjoy all your little conversations. You will be healing and connecting on so many levels, and peace will follow into your heart, mind, body and soul.

 *Love&Light*

TRUTH

"Be true and just be you."
You are being guided to see, feel and know the truth.
You are a ray of light from God. A wondrous soul and
being; know this truth, hold this truth, and be at peace
with this truth.
Live this TRUTH.

✿ ₹ گ ʕ ˜˜ ಲ *Love&Light*

FREE

You are free, no matter what: God wants you to know this as true. Your right to be free is within you, it is in fact a choice, your choice. Release all your fears and worries to him. You are safe, trust in God. Release is to be free, you can set yourself free; choose to be free now. Know that you are so much more than anything negative. Set yourself FREE.

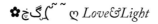 ♥ *Love&Light*

BELIEVE

Trust your inner knowledge. Listen to the voice within. Your faith is your belief and your belief is your faith. It is time to work with your inner self. Know that you are capable of achieving all your desires. Take hold of your soul's knowledge of truth, what you can think you can do. BELIEVE in you and your dreams will come true.

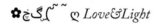 *Love&Light*

SOUL

The angels are asking you to look within and see the true essence of your being. Your soul is strong. It is your fire. It speaks to you in the moments of just being and through your first thoughts and gut feelings. Pull your body, mind and soul together and be all you can be in love and light. Give your soul a chance to lead you to your spiritual enlightenment. Your SOUL has wisdom beyond the mind's ability to understand, but not beyond your reach if you start to listen.

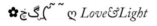 *Love&Light*

GRATITUDE

Living in gratitude brings you closer to you, closer to your divine purpose and closer to your dreams. You see, being grateful for all you have, little things, big things, children, family, pets, friends, everything, brings you more of the like. Why? Because you are focusing on all the good you have in your life. You are rising above anything that is going wrong. When you are in a state of gratitude you are in a state of just being; a truly wonderful and natural state. You get to see you and your world in all its glory. You embrace all that is true and right and you welcome more of the same. To live in GRATITUDE is to live in the divine and being grateful for simply being alive.

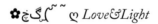 ♥ *Love&Light*

JESUS

To see life and see you as Jesus sees you is to truly have understood the simple meaning of it all. Whatever the name JESUS means to you or however you choose to use your faith and belief in all that is in love and light. The meaning is one, of ever-living and ever-loving energy, Divine sacrifice for you and for all. This is your guiding star and universal invitation to give it all away, and release it all. Hand over everything that weighs you down. Give yourself the sense of relief that will come from knowing that all is being taken care of, and by asking for help and handing it over. You were created to be happy and that's all the divine energy ever wants for you. Honour yourself by taking that shoulder to lean on, release all fear and negativity so you can live as you were meant to live. Be at peace dear soul, all is ok.

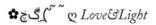 *Love&Light*

NATURE

It is time to come back to the world of nature. You are being asked to remember how wonderful being outside makes you feel! Take a walk, sit out and read a book; anything. Breathe in the fresh air. Look all around you and try for the moments you are with nature, to switch off and just be. JUST BE in the moment. You are nature and nature is you, try to come home to your natural state, which is peace and happiness. Out in NATURE is a wonderful way to remind yourself of your divine state.

❀ چگ‌ۺ﮲ ʕ˜ ˜ ღ *Love&Light*

WINGS

Spread your wings and fly high. You have been graced with so many gifts and talents that the world is your oyster. Set aside anything that others may say to put you down. Set aside anything your Ego may try to throw in front of you in fear. You are your own master; you have all the power within that is needed to achieve your dreams. You are safe and protected from above on your journey so take flight and use your divine WINGS to bring you to the life you truly seek.

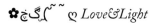 *Love&Light*

MIRROR

Now it is time to take time for you and the reason being is to look again and look deeper at yourself, with a kind but questioning heart as to what it is that you do not like about your life and you as it stands now. But Mirror can also mean: be a mirror for traits in others that you do like and see that you can be that too. Then try mirroring out the parts of your soul that you do like. Reflect to others what you like about them and you. So that you start to see those wonderful things more and think about them more: Then the habit of living well and loving you and others as they truly are will start to MIRROR from you forever more.

✿چگ؟˜ ♡ *Love&Light*

FIRE

Fire is your passion; it is time to awaken it or at least to stop ignoring it. You have the power to make time in your day to fuel your fire AKA Soul. A happy soul is well fuelled and fed. It is this that gives you the fire for life and the fire to inspire others too. Light your FIRE.

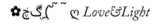 Love&Light

READ

READ is a gentle hint to take some time out and pamper your imagination with a good book. Or fuel your fire and soul with some new knowledge. Switching off and distracting your brain with something like a book is a wonderful way to get answers. It works in the same way the "if you can't think of a name" scenario does... When you stop trying to think of it the name always come to you? Let your brain and subconscious do some work, you relax and switch off by doing something enjoyable and it will find your answers.

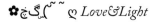 *Love&Light*

GROUNDED

Grounded is to do something to re ground yourself. Take a walk or open some windows, something that will bring you back to the earth and settle your emotions. Come back to the beginning to find answers and peace. Back to nature and ground your thoughts. Imagine roots growing from your feet and working their way down through mother earth and stabilising you to the ground with the love from God and Earth. To GROUND yourself is to allow answers and inner happiness and peace to flow. Come back to your natural state.

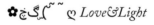 Love&Light

PERSPECTIVE

Everything in life happens for a reason, and sometimes we find it hard to see why things may happen. This is normal and a true human process and this is ok, you're being asked to try to step outside the box and see the bigger picture. See things as a whole. The funny thing is, to change your perspective of the outside; you need to bring everything back to the self, change your view of you and you will see the world differently automatically. You are loved, guided and protected so it is safe for you to really love and see you in a different PERSPECTIVE. This is where the true change happens.

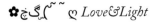 *Love&Light*

STOP

Stop tends to mean, that you need to STOP... take time to see your world and your life. Do not just enjoy a time of your life in the memory of it because you were too busy or worried to enjoy it while it was happening. It is in your power to stop and see your life unfold and enjoy each and every moment as it happens. And then yes, through this you will also have more powerful memories with no hidden guilt that you didn't enjoy it then and there. Live strong, live vibrant and JUST LIVE.

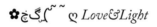 *Love&Light*

CHANNEL

You are always divinely protected and guided and it is within this guidance that you can CHANNEL all the wonders of the universe and God. You know all you need to know, it is now time to channel that inner beauty and knowledge by listening to you and all that is spiritual within. You will always be receiving help and more information, so honour your God given right to channel tranquil and inspirational messages to the world. You choose your medium for this channelling, and all pathways will open for you.

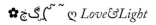 *Love&Light*

EMBRACE

Shout out with joy that you are ALIVE. It is time for you to truly see the love and wonder that is you. Throw away all those Ego made shackles and should do's. You are a divine being of light from God. EMBRACE all that is you, all and everything exactly as you are. Forgive and release. Cherish your lessons, live your truth and embrace the life that is completely as it should be right now. Rejoice along your path towards your life purpose. Every moment is a new moment, so embrace it all and truly shine.

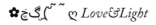 *Love&Light*

RESPECT

The greatest gift you will award yourself is to love and respect yourself truly and totally. From the gift of love of self and the respect of self, you can truly see others as God sees them. You can offer all the respect and love that those dear to you deserve and beam this respect out to the entire universe and all its creations familiar or not. From gratitude of all you have: will come that tranquil peace that comes from being happy now: Being happy with your life, with you and even your flaws, comes a divine respect and love of self that you are being urged to grace yourself with. Treat yourself kindly, forgive yourself. Know you are a wonderful being and deserve your unshakable RESPECT for the self.

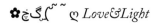 ♔ چگ ڈ ~ ~ ♀ *Love&Light*

GROW

This is a very powerful and spiritual time in your earthly existence and within the universe. This is the time to shine, spread your wings and grow to your full potential. You are divine and in the likeness of your maker. Rise above all your body bound beliefs and honour your true self and soul and see the stunning real truth of your spirit and heavenly abilities. Your power is within you, your power to be a beacon of love, guidance and light. To hold true to all that is created from love and grace and embrace all you meet with the same. You are extremely important to the growth of all mankind and this earth. See you and others as God sees you, spread this sight and GROW from within in the power that is unconditional love.

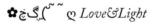 *Love&Light*

HEIGHTS

This is a gentle nudge to rise now to the heights you have always dreamed of. No idea or wish is too big or too small. You are in line with your destiny for great heights. You are a magnificent being. Now is your window to rise to your divine heights.

❀ چگ ڒ ˜ ˜ ♡ *Love&Light*

CALM

You know in your heart of hearts that all is well and just as it should be. Release all fear and negativity as you no longer need it. You are being asked to truly trust and release. All is well and you are on the right path. To see and feel your next moves you need to stay calm within, listen to the silence. From this calm will come all answers as your soul knows them already and is trying to tell you always; be still, be CALM and all will become clear!

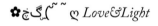 ♥ *Love&Light*

MOVE

In these great times of spiritual movement you are being wrapped in white light and asked to move inward and upward. See the real you, love you and be you. Movement towards the divine being you are is of paramount importance in the coming years. Lift up and be happy now, shine and share your love now. Help others see the true meaning of gratitude and spiritual love and living. Move towards the greatest you, you have all the help you need from above, just ask and roads will light up for you. So MOVE towards your dreams and trust that everything in your way will move as your confidence and determination grows. Your life and the universe are all about movement. Take time to just be and flow like the tide, breathe in your divine and eternal movement. The harmonious flow and movement of life is yours.

✿ چگ ܦ ~ ~ ღ *Love&Light*

HOPE

This is one of your most powerful gifts and defences. Against all odds hope will prevail. Hope is not a ticket to sit back and wait, but it is your card to success and a driving force towards the completion of your divine purpose. You see, within you is a light and it is ever shining, this beacon will guide you and stir you through all waters. This light, this HOPE is your inner wisdom and true faith. Using its guidance you will never go wrong, all will map out as it should do and you should never fear, this HOPE is the love and light from God and it is within your very being. Your hope is the knowledge that you can do and achieve it all.

❀چگ ¸ ~~ ♡ *Love&Light*

ASK

The one thing you need to hold true is that you are never alone, this journey of yours is surrounded in love and light and everything you will ever need to shine and complete is here now. However, the one thing most of us miss is that, all our needs will be met, all the help is there, all the signs are being given and all the God winks are being shown... you just need to ASK and then see. Ask God and the angels into your life, voice to them your needs and wishes, talk to them, they will help you as they see fit, all will work out in divine order exactly as it should do, but remember the power lies with you. You need to ASK.

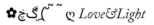 *Love&Light*

TRANQUILITY

The search for tranquillity is something that unites all souls across the whole universe. The wonderful news is that you are in charge of creating and living your own tranquillity. We come back to the self in times of gratitude and happiness. Your true natural state is happiness. If you take the time daily to JUST BE, and see your world, listen to your body, come back to your breath, feel the life within you and things will clear. Slow and calm down, you will find the inner happiness, the feeling of pure tranquil peace. This feeling will automatically flow from the realisation of gratitude, for everything and everyone in your world. Simply put, be happy now, be thankful now, being all these things NOW is being tranquil, you will feel the divine ease of TRANQUILLITY wash over you when you release all negativity and choose to be happy and tranquil now. All is perfect and just as it should be. Breathe!

✿چگ٢ ˜ ღ Love&Light

SEE

You are being asked raise your strength, faith and vibrations. God sees you and he wants you to see you and others as he does; in love and divine light. Your soul knows this truth. Honour your true being by seeing yourself as you really are. Love you, forgive you, and SEE you. A whole new world is waiting for you to just see.

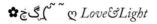 *Love&Light*

ABUNDANCE

The abundance we all seek is a funny being! We are fever rich in abundance of all sorts, to find the abundance you seek you must first acknowledge the abundance you already have. Listen to on high, you will see, you are rich beyond belief. When you truly feel this within, then you can move forth and attract more. Law of attraction states; like begets like, taking this into account you will learn: If you see and honour your abundance now you will attract more. You are in control of what comes your way, you just have to see it now, think it now and know that against all odds, because you think it, it will come. ABUNDANCE means many things to many people, find out what is means to you and think it now!

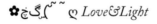 *Love&Light*

NAMASTE

Long story short, not in the exact words of its original origin:

I see your soul!

You are being urged to see you and others as they are. See the very energy that connects us all; honour the oneness! Really see your soul and see the souls of others. With grace, look within you and others, beyond all earthly thoughts. Try not to judge, try not to pretend to know or understand what they see or feel, Just see you and others in the divine energy that you and they are created from. NAMASTE!

✿ ﺝﻙﻝ ~ ℘ Love&Light

BRIGHT

You are on your way. Yes keep that tune in your heart. That tune is making you bright, making your light shine even on the darkest of days. All is being taken care of; all you need to do is follow your heart. It is time to throw away all fear and all doubt, you are on your way. You are ready, you are on the right path and you are beating earth's heart beat. Go now and be bright, be you, let the world see your unique BRIGHT light.

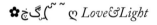 *Love&Light*

PLAY

This is a warrior angel message for you, calling for you to recall that inner child. The child that never gave up, the child that loved all and lived all and would play through all. You see, as we grow, we learn new lessons and gain knowledge, however this is a reminder that some of the knowledge and inner strength we were born with was meant to stay, meant to be part of our grown up lives. That strength, that soldier-like vibrancy combined with no fear that we all played with in youth was one of the things that was supposed to stay! Recall your play, recall yourself, find that child that was stronger than some parts of you are now and play there. Recall, relive, laugh, and remember the freedom and strength of your innocent youth where all was possible just because it was PLAY!

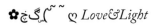 ♥ *Love&Light*

SEIZE

See right now, this is your time! You are feeling things and you are longing for growth. This is your time to move on and take the leap of faith. All things and signs for you show that you need to seize this time in your life. Seize your moment. Live! Take the risk! Jump forth and run like the wind towards all you see and feel for you. Take this moment in time, be all you can be. Charge forward; you are being backed up and followed from above. Raise your flag and SEIZE your dreams!

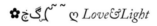 ♡ *Love&Light*

SUCCESS

Rising above all odds and all negativity! Your light shines through! Go on, go forth and be all you can be. Succeed in all areas, truly be you and truly shine. No matter what comes your way you will always make lemonade from lemons. You are here to be all you can be and you are being this and more, and always have been. You will always hear an inner tune and calling that will let you fly and achieve, no matter what; you have already made it! You are backed up with the divine, you are guided and you are armed with the tools! What may lie ahead is up to you! Just always believe in your SUCCESS!

❀څگ୮~~ ౧ *Love&Light*

HEALING

Healing is a mystical energy that breaths in every living thing. A profound miracle worker, which can cure the physical and spiritual parts of all beings, we are all healers and gifted with the white light that can crash through boundaries and rise above all obstacles. HEALING begins within, releasing all to forgiveness and light. Letting go of earthly worries and embracing the belief that all is ok. Healing is a power that you have always had within your core, never fear when you may hurt or feel any of the lower energies, you will rise above and heal once you love yourself unconditionally, be kind to yourself and know that positive energy, time and patience heals all wounds.

❀چگٍ ͡ ͠ ♥ *Love&Light*

FEAR

Like all emotions, the feeling of fear has been given to us to arm us in life. As we have moved along our journey somehow we have forgotten its real purpose and it has grown into an emotion no longer desired by us. You see; fear was given as a tool, fight or flight. To be used as a guidance system deeply rooted within our gut, to navigate us through times of trouble. You are being asked to respect the emotion but remember that FEAR is only a tool, an instantaneous tip from the gut that all many not be as it should be in a situation. You control fear and that tip from within, and you can decide when you need it and when to us it to move you away from negative things. It is your tool to use on your terms, let it work for you not paralyse you. When controlled and understood, fear can be another link that makes your armour even stronger.

❀چگ‍ؐ ˜ ღ *Love&Light*

HONEST

Powerful and wise are you when living in honesty. Honour your soul by always coming back to a state of truth. From this place of honesty you will find the road to your life purpose. You will find the real and everlasting connection of life within all your relationships. You will find answers to any problems. As you move through this wonderful life, always remember being honest to yourself and remembering what you stand for is a huge element in the foundations of peace. Peace will beam through you as stand up and be HONEST to you.

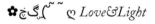 ♡ *Love&Light*

SERENDIPITY

Love and hugs from above are gathering around you now. All things wonderful that seem accidental are no accident. They are signs and divine guides, all pointing you to the life of your dreams. You are being reminded to be very aware of the world and all that is happening right now. Everything is linking together in a collage of uplifting events that will whirlwind round, with you at the eye. This is your time to be spontaneous and follow these signs. Your angels are with you and will support you in this new and exciting life that is unfolding for you. SERENDIPITY is the key to your life purpose.

✿ چگ⸂˜ ♡ *Love&Light*

CHERISH

Cherish every moment and everyone in that moment. Gratitude will lead you to the things you will cherish. You have been led to places on your path for a reason. All lessons, all happiness, all loved ones have a divine meaning in your personal journey. Open you heart like a lotus flower and embrace all you have, thunder through your life in love and light leaving no room for regret. If you CHERISH the very essences of every person and moment you will never stumble onto the longer path. You will thrive and grow ever more.

❀ چگ ۵ ~ ♡ *Love&Light*

GOD

I always feel that this is always a gentle reminder that you are not alone, and I feel that it is that He has heard you and your thoughts. Love and light will hold you high and strong, just ask Him. Never forget to ask Him... God will not mess with free will so you need to ask Him. This is also a hug to help you not to let doubt creep in, to stay in Faith and hope. It is His way of holding out His hands and saying "Give it all to me". LET GO AND LET GOD

❀چگ‌ٱ˜ ~ ♡ *Love&Light*

ABOUT THE AUTHOR

LESLEY MCKEEVER is an artist, photographer, designer, energy healer and spiritual writer who lives by the sea in her native County Dublin. Lesley is a people person but not all of her "people" have their feet on the ground for they are angels and on her walk through this spiritual journey of growth and enlightenment she is assured of their presence. She has a deep unbreakable love and faith with and within God to whom she hands over everything in her life daily. She combines an interest in the ethereal with the practical skills of IT by which she supports her one very tolerant daughter who vies for affection with an aged St Bernard and a young St Dane, two cats and any stray that lands at her door. Her love of horses has been a lifelong passion often expressed in her paintings. Scraps for scraps may not describe mealtimes but there is no doubting who has the bigger appetite in this ménage!

MORE TO COME FROM THE AUTHOR

Keep your eyes peeled for all future publications from Lesley McKeever.

Such as

Positivity Echoes, VII©

On the Wings of Affirmations V I©

Soul Angel Meditations VI©

White Light Healing Quotes VI©

Soul for Life ©

White Light Soul Healing Tasks ©

Soul Angel and Energy Healing Angel Card Decks ©

For more information contact

soulhealing@live.ie or Facebook: Soul Angel and Energy Healing

RIP

BERNARD

17th Sept 2003– 18th June 2012.

Goodbye to our beloved Bernard. The gentle giant, with the heart of gold.
Who has left us with such comforting memories of joy, love and faithful togetherness! Thank you for our time together all those wonderful years from who we called fluppy puppy to wise and strong aged soul uncle Berno. Your very being and spirit was a guiding light and an honour to know. A pure divine example of Love and Peace for us all to live by! Loved and cuddled by so many, we will never forget the time and love you had for us all. Please remember, we and I will always think of you and be happy, for you are at peace and safe with God. I saw your soul from the moment I meet you as you saw mine. A kindred spirit bond, which will walk with me forever!
Living with you has been an honour I will cherish all my life. I love you beyond belief. To you my Bernard, I know you are with us, as are hearts and memories are with you, Maddie and I Love you forever and for always.